CW01066833

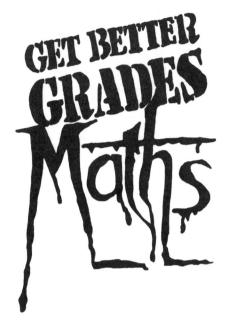

GET BETTER GRADES

GRADES

Maths

GET BETTER GRADES

GRADES

Maths

Margie Agnew   Steve Barlow
Owen Davies   Steve
Lee Pascal   Skidmore

Piccadilly Press • London

Printed and bound by WBC, Bridgend
for the publishers Piccadilly Press Ltd.,
5 Castle Road, London NW1 8PR

A catalogue record for this book is available from the British Library

ISBN: 1 85340 392 X (trade paperback)
1 85340 387 3 (hardback)

Margie Agnew lives in West London. She teaches in a comprehensive school and has been involved in Study Skills courses for students and training courses for teachers.

Steve Barlow lives is a teacher who lives in Heanor, Derbyshire. He has written several books in collaboration with Steve Skidmore including I FELL IN LOVE WITH A LEATHER JACKET, IN LOVE WITH AN URBAN GORILLA and, coming soon, ACTION REPLAYS.

Owen Davies lives in West London. He is a maths teacher in a comprehensive school.

Lee Pascal lives in Richmond, Surrey. He lectures on Writing and Study Skills in secondary schools. He is also a Special Needs teacher with particular interest in Dyslexia.

Steve Skidmore lives in Leicestershire. He spends his time teaching, writing and watching Leicester Tigers. He met Steve Barlow while teaching in Nottingham and they began writing together.

Designed by Zena Flax

C O N T E N T S

INTRODUCTION	7
CONFIDENCE	8
GOLDEN RULES	10
CALCULATOR	12
FRACTIONS	20
NUMBER PATTERNS	23
NEGATIVE NUMBERS	27
TIME	28
SIGNIFICANT FIGURES	29
ALGEBRA	32
COMMON FACTORS	35
SHAPES	36
ALGEBRA (again)	42
ANGLES	44
SCALE	48
RATIO	54
POWERS	58
STANDARD FORM	60
CIRCLES	63
PYTHAGORAS	69
SYMMETRY	77
BEARINGS	79
AREA	81
VOLUME	84
(Yet More) ALGEBRA	85
SEQUENCES	88
PROBABILITY	90
CHARTS AND GRAPHS	93
REFERENCE SECTION	96
INDEX	

We all (Margie, Lee and the two Steves) met in Lee's house in London.

Apparently, Steve Skidmore had some news.

"Piccadilly Press called," he began. "They wanted to talk about *Get Better Grades*..."

"How's it selling?" we asked.

"Like hot cakes, apparently. The point is," he went on, "they want us to do another one."

"Another one?"

"ON MATHS."

There was a stunned silence. Then everyone started talking at once.

Lee said there were primitive tribes in the Amazon rain forest who couldn't count above three. Their counting system went, 'One, two, three ... *lots*'. Even so, they were better at maths than him.

Skidmore said he couldn't count up to twenty without taking his shoes and socks off. Barlow said *he* couldn't count up to twenty without taking his shoes *and* socks off and using a calculator.

Margie looked thoughtful. Then she said she knew a really nice guy called Owen who was brilliant at maths. Should she give him a ring?

"YES!!!!!!" we chorused.

When Owen met us, he didn't seem to think it strange to be planning a study skills book in maths with a group of people whose grasp of mathematical principles could have been bettered by a goldfish.

"Our being useless at maths might even be a good thing," mused Margie.

We asked her how she reckoned that.

"Well, let's face it," she said, "if we can write a book that explains maths so that we can understand it, then **ANYBODY** will be able to understand it!"

We looked at each other. "That's true," we said.

So we wrote the book, and here it is.

CONFIDENCE MAKE OVER

Our Health and Beauty consultant, Kay Sera-Serah, exclusively reveals her Top Tips for Maths Confidence.

Follow Kay's unique **M-Plan Diet** for
Better, More Accurate Results.

 BREAKFAST

Don't start your day with anything too heavy. If you try tackling a huge fry-up of Trigonometry and Binomial Theorems first thing in the morning, you won't fancy anything else for the rest of the day! Start with something lighter, and keep yourself going with bite-sized nibbles during the day!

LUNCH

I know people who stuff themselves with facts, then need a three-hour nap. Take it easy! You won't get any satisfaction from wolfing down loads of information at one sitting. Always get up from your lunch study feeling you could take in a little more!

 DINNER

A romantic candle-lit study (if there's a power cut) is fine, but don't overdo it! People who try to gorge into the small hours just end up with mental indigestion and heartburn.

Try the M-Plan Diet: little and often is the rule!

GET BETTER GRADES HEADCURE

for perfect, healthy, shining maths WHATEVER your type!

● ● ●

Flyaway:

Can't keep your mind on formulae? Can't organise figures? **Get Better Grades Headcure** helps you keep in mind those troublesome concepts, and mend split ends!

Greasy:

Do formulae slip from your memory? Can't keep hold of figures? **Get Better Grades Headcure** gives you control and body!

Dry:

Bored and listless with dry mathematical formulae? Our fun tips keep you interested. Don't do your head in, use **Get Better Grades Headcure** for a healthy sheen.

Read on . . . . the next page should solve your confidence problem!!

The Golden Rules rule O.K?

•The•Four•

ADDITION

•sums are done from right to left

$$123$$
$$+123$$

•the total is always bigger than both numbers

$$246 \impliedby \text{Start}$$

Other words used for addition:

→ the sum of
→ plus
→ the outcome
→ altogether

SUBTRACTION

•always go from right to left

$$468$$
$$-246$$

•the total is smaller than the biggest number

$$222 \impliedby \text{Start}$$

Other words used for subtraction:

→ take away
→ subtract
→ find the difference
→ minus

•Golden•Rules•

MULTIPLICATION

- •always goes from right to left

$$468$$
$$\times\ \ 6$$

- •always gets bigger if the multiple is bigger than 1

$$2008\ \ \Leftarrow Start$$

Other words used for multiplication:

→ times

→ what is the product?

DIVISION

- •always gets smaller
- •always goes from **left** to **right** Start

$$2$$
$$Start \Rightarrow 50\ \overline{)100}$$

Other words used for division:

→ share

→ divide

→ quotient

REMEMBER: Most maths skills involve the

•Four•Golden•Rules•

One author's note: As I'm the world's worst mathematician this makes me feel **GOOD!** Even I can add, divide, subtract and multiply!

Calculate your future:

Clarence, our *GET BETTER GRADES* astrologer, has been staring at his crystal ball again to show how your star sign can influence your approach to maths and, in particular, to your calculator.

Hint: Calculators differ. **Keep the instruction booklet that comes with the calculator.** As you need more and more functions, refer to the booklet and take one step at a time. In your horoscope, names for buttons should be easy to find in the instruction booklet. If not, **ask your maths teacher.**

ARIES

March 21 - April 20

Yes Aries, we know. Being strong-willed and a born leader, you want EVERYTHING out of life and everything out of your calculator. The **Second Function button** is an absolute must for you. Press it to give you a whole new world of fancy functions. You'll see your function options written in small letters above or below the main buttons. Check your instruction booklet for the name that they give to the **second function button.** Once you've mastered this button Aries, the calculator will hold nothing back from you.

TAURUS

April 21 - May 21

Rush, rush, rush, and mess it all up. You've done it before, haven't you, Taurus? O.K. this time slow down a bit and make sure that you're not making really silly mistakes with your calculator. (First of all, check to see how your calculator tackles this sum: **4 + 2 x 3.**) This is really important because a cheap calculator that puts numbers in from left to right won't do **BODMAS** (see Scorpio). **Left to right calculators give the answer 18.** Then, make sure that you don't commit two of the most common Taurus errors: ignoring the decimal point or, when adding pounds and pence, instead of putting in **72 pence** as **.72** putting it in as **72** and getting a completely outrageous answer.

GEMINI

May 22 - June 21

What a changeable sort you are, never sticking to one thing at a time, always going backwards and forwards aren't you? Well, now's the time to put this habit to the test and learn how to use your **plus/minus button.** I know that minus numbers are still magic to you (see page 26), but with your calculator, all you have to do is press this super button to change the number from a **plus number to a minus number.** As you usually change your mind after you've done something, it will be easy for you to remember to use this button **after** you've chosen the number and it is displayed on the screen.

CANCER

June 22 - July 23

I know, Cancer, it's always someone else's fault. If a mistake comes up on your calculator, it has to be a problem with the stupid machine, not that you could have possibly keyed in the wrong number or the wrong function. Look Cancer, it's time to stop blaming others for the errors and check out how you are approaching the machine. Remember when you first got the calculator and your divisions always came out wrong, and it took you three hours to discover that to divide **27 by 3** you don't key in **3 ÷ 27** but **27 ÷ 3**? Wise up Cancer, key in the correct information and you'll always get the right answer.

LEO

July 24 - August 23

Oh dear, oh dear. Impetuous fool you, so impatient, so much in a hurry to get on with things. In fact, you're wasting a great deal of time with your impatience, always getting angry with yourself and your calculator if you make a mistake. Relax Leo, you can save yourself hours of work if you don't use that $\boxed{AC}$ button every time you mess up. How many times have you added up a column of 127 numbers, keyed in a six instead of a nine, said, "Oh my goodness," (well your seven year old sister might pick up this book) cancelled out all of your work and started over again. Well, Leo, you don't have to do that! Just push the $\boxed{C/CE}$ (get out the magnifying glass and check your instruction booklet to find out which button it is) and simply cancel out your **last** number.

VIRGO

August 24 - September 23

Methodical, calm, taking everything step by step and usually getting the right answers - boy Virgo, do you ever get on people's nerves! However, you could add a dash of excitement to your life by using the **fraction button**. I know, you prefer the old-fashioned, dreary way of multiplying the top numbers and then multiplying the bottom numbers to work out a fraction multiplication; however, it's much more fun and **time saving** if you simply use the fraction button in place of the dividing line. You can also save yourself time by **converting fractions to decimals** by simply **dividing** the top number by the lower number to give the decimal equivalent instead of using the old fashioned method of multiplying the fraction by a hundred. Come on Virgo, get some lead in your batteries and use your buttons!

LIBRA

September 24 - October 23

What a fusspot! You really tend to complicate things by trying to work with a whole series of numbers, keeping them in your head or constantly referring to them on the maths question, keying them in repeatedly and getting really worked up with the amount of time that all these processes are taking. Help is at hand, Libra, with the use of the memory buttons. If you need to divide a series of numbers by the same sum, put the sum into memory with the **Min** button and pull it out when you need it with the **MR** button. The buttons could also be called **STO** for Store and **REC** for Recall. These little buttons will save you hours of tedious repetitive operations, and give you more time to spend on sticking those three thousand stamps into your stamp album, or standing in the High Street jotting down bus numbers.

SCORPIO

October 24 - November 22

Ouch Scorpio - dashing from place to place with a vicious sting in your tail! I know that you think it's productive to whizz around without planning your route, and maybe you think that you're incapable of organizing yourself to do things in a structured way. Well, Scorpio, dashing around will get you into trouble because maths is about structure and order, but help is at hand. **BODMAS** (see page 19) is a clever little device **built into your calculator** to organize your maths problems. In order to over-ride **BODMAS**, you'll have to use your brackets buttons to separate your problem from the **BODMAS** feature. Put groups of numbers within brackets (you can add, subtract, multiply or divide **within** the brackets), and then solve your problem with another set of bracketed figures.

SAGITTARIUS

November 23 - December 21

O.K. Sagittarius, you know **everything**. Or at least, you may not always arrive at the correct answer, but you present the wrong one with great conviction! You seem to have this bug in your head constantly saying **"over-ride, over-ride"** and when you do, you end up in deep trouble. You do it with the cancel button (see Leo), with BODMAS (have a chat with a Scorpio), but most of all you do it with the standard form button. **Stop over-riding this button by multiplying the answer by ten!** If you ever multiply by 10, as well as using the EXP or EE button again, watch out for a bolt of lightning to strike you the next time Mars lines up with Uranus. (See also page 60 for more details.)

CAPRICORN

December 22 - January 20

Get to the point, Capricorn! You do go on, don't you? ON and ON and ON. Listen up Capri, you're going to bore yourself to death with all that button pushing. You have a brilliant option of using the Powers button. Next time, instead of typing in 9 x 9 x 9 twelve times to figure out **9** to the power of **12**, just key in **9,** then the **powers button**, x^y then 12 to get the right answer. Next we'll have to teach you to use the **x** button to multiply 127 by 341 instead of keying in 127 three hundred and forty one times!

AQUARIUS

January 21 - February 19

Yes, you're calm. Yes, you're tranquil. Yes, you're orderly. But aren't you the teensiest bit worried that others might think that you're just a bit square? Loosen up, kid, and use a bit of calculator magic to improve your image. No more will the others have to watch you going through the tedious step of **multiplying 64 by 64** to arrive at the answer. Put your tables aside and discover the joys of the square button. Just push this little marvel and watch the right answer appear on your screen. Try the same for square roots and cube roots and, when it comes time for you to join **The Magic Circle** (see page 63) you'll be one step ahead.

PISCES

February 20 - March 20

Oh what a sense of humour! Yes, Pisces, maths is fun, but stop taking the Pisces out of your calculator! Trying to fool it by pushing in the wrong series of instructions isn't going to get you anywhere (take a look at Scorpio to see what I mean). You, however, have this really annoying habit of pushing the four basic function buttons (**x + - ÷**) in a random fashion, and expecting the machine to remember your order. Sorry Pisces, your calculator doesn't share your stunning wit. It only remembers and acts upon your **last** instruction. So carry on pushing; your calculator will cancel out **all** your old instructions and only work the most recent one.

B O D M A S

Here is a quick rule to help you remember the order of the Golden Rules and Brackers.

B	**O**	**D**	**M**	**A**	**S**
R	F	I	U	D	U
A		V	L	D	B
C		I	T	I	T
K		S	I	T	R
E		I	P	I	A
T		O	L	O	C
S		N	I	N	T
			C		I
			A		O
			T		N
			I		
			O		
			N		

So, if you want to find the answer to **3 + 4 x 6** = you do the multiplication before the addition. This makes the answer 27.

Why? Because **4 x 6 = 24** (the multiplication) and
 3 + 24 = 27 (the addition).
Here's another example: **5 x (7 + 6 ÷ 2)**.

You look at the part in brackets first **(7 - 6 ÷ 2)**. From BODMAS do division before subtraction so
 6 ÷ 2 = 3 then
 7 - 3 = 4.
 Now multiply this answer by **5** from the example
 5 x (4) = 20.

HINT: MDF calculators follow BODMAS (see page 13).

MATHEMATICAL GENIUS EINSTEIN ANSWERS YOUR NUMERIC NIGHTMARES!

Dear Einstein*,
I am very very frightened of fractions. Is it really true that when you multiply fractions they get <u>smaller</u>?? Why? Help!
Yours, Muddled.

Dear Muddled,

Now can you calm down and listen? Multiplying fractions is easy! Multiply top to top and bottom to bottom. For example:

$$\tfrac{1}{2} \times \tfrac{1}{2} = \tfrac{1}{4}$$

Let me give you some advice.
The first is general:

Always work out fractions with a calculator unless you happen to be doing your exams on a desert island.

Give yourself a crash course in the use of a calculator for fractions. There is a weird button that looks like $\boxed{a \ b/c}$ which is pretty **key** to the whole thing.

Love, **Einstein**

P.S. Aren't you glad that I didn't ask you to cut up an orange or divide a pizza just like all those maths examiners do!?

*Not Albert Einstein, the famous genius, but Adrian Einstein, mathematical genius.✱✱

✱✱Well actually, he mends bikes for a living, but he's dead good at maths, honest!

FRACTIONS

Dear Perplexed,

A very challenging question. Since we seem vaguely to be on the topic of fractions, I reckon that your teacher has hit on something pretty good. You know how if we dug a big hole we would get to Australia and that everything there is upside down because it is the other side of the world? You also know that day is night and night is day and that the bath water goes down the plug hole circling the opposite way from ours? Well, that sort of upside down, change me round chaos is reflected in **dividing** fractions.

This is what you do: You turn the second fraction upside down and then you multiply instead of divide,

$$eg \quad \frac{3}{4} \div \frac{4}{7} = \frac{3}{4} \times \frac{7}{4} = \frac{21}{16}$$

Love, **Einstein**

Dear Einstein,

The Australian bit was brilliant. But . . . you've guessed it. What about adding and subtracting these fractions??

Love, Getting-more-Confident

Dear Getting-more-Confident,

It's like this: If you are adding or subtracting you just do it to the top line and leave the bottom alone.

For example, $\frac{1}{5} + \frac{3}{5} = \frac{4}{5}$

It's not too bad especially if the bottom line is the same. If it isn't, ask your teacher to explain about lowest common denominators.

Love, **Einstein**

Dear Einstein,

I am 0.75, $\frac{3}{4}$ or 75% sure about decimals, fractions and percentages but I still have a problem changing decimals into fractions. Help!

Love, Justine Bits

Dear Justine Bits,

It's a doddle!

1 figure after the point goes over 10 i.e. $0.2 = \frac{2}{10}$

2 figures after the point goes over 100 i.e. $0.50 = \frac{50}{100}$

3 figures after the point goes over 1000 i.e. $0.236 = \frac{236}{1000}$

You can then cancel them down!

Love, **Einstein**

NUMBER PATTERNS

You need to know about number patterns for your exams. The reason they are included in the syllabus is because they teach you how to **manipulate** numbers. Knowing about number patterns will help you to become a more flexible and mathematical thinker.

Here are eight types of number sequences you should recognise:

Better Grades Tip: Look in the gaps between the numbers - it will usually help you to identify a pattern.

I. EVEN NUMBERS: (2 x table)

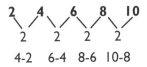

4-2   6-4   8-6   10-8

2. ODD NUMBERS: (those not divisible by 2)

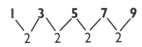

3. PRIME NUMBERS:

Facts:

i) They don't divide by anything except themselves and 1

ii) They don't crop up in tables

Rules to find if a number is a **Prime Number:**

i) must end in 1, 3, 7 or 9 (sod's law: ones that do end in those numbers may not be Prime Numbers).

ii) make sure it's not divisible by 3 or 7.

ii) exceptions: 2 and 5 at the beginning.

The first Prime Numbers are:

2   3   5   7   11   13   17   19   23   29   31

Note: There is no gap pattern.

4. SQUARE NUMBERS:

Facts: You need to know your tables or have a calculator. Square numbers are those that multiply themselves.

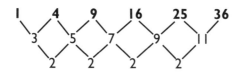

Note: The gap pattern only emerges in the third row.

5. TRIANGLE NUMBERS:

Think of stacking baked bean tins.

Pattern: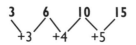

Note: Each new row has one more can.

6. STEADY DIFFERENCE TYPE:

(adding)   8   11   15   20   26
              3   4   5   6

Note: gaps are going up in ones.

(subtracting)   74   64   55   47   40
                  -10   -9   -8   -7

Note: gaps are going down by one each time.

7a. MULTIPLYING FACTOR TYPE:

5   10   20   40
  x2   x2   x2

x 2 each number - you get the same result if you look at the gaps.

7b. DIVIDING FACTOR TYPE:

320   80   20   5

Note: each number is divided by 4.

8. ADDING PREVIOUS TERMS TYPE:

This is the last of them. All the other sequences have been honest sequence types, but figure people love playing so they sometimes dream up other sequences such as this one:

1   1   2   3   5   8   13   21

No gap pattern. What they have done is added:

$$1 + 1 = 2$$
$$1 + 2 = 3$$
$$2 + 3 = 5$$

This is tricky because you have to scan backwards!

Dear Einstein,
  I never understand why two minuses equal a plus.
Yours, Confused.

Dear Confused,
  As it happens I can help you: it is just like "my calculator don't have no batteries" i.e. it **has** batteries. Beware, this only works if the minuses are together. For example:
  $3 - (-8) = 3 + 8 = 11$
  Love, **Einstein.**

Dear Einstein,
  I don't think you're a genius even if you did get into that relativity bit. You completely failed to tell me that plus minus is the same as minus. Let me explain: If I have to work out my finances which are **£5** (mine) plus **minus £3** (what I owe Mum) unfortunately I am left with **£2.00**. Or to put it more mathematically, **5 + (-3) = 2**. So we needn't have the plus at all. It could just be **5-3**. Haa!
  Yours, Not-So-Confused

Dear Not-So-Confused,

You're learning. I thought that was far too hard for you. The way I look at it is that in this life it never rains but it pours, i.e. **the minus is more powerful than the plus** . . . Typical! By the way, remember that these little calculations only work like this when you are doing adding and subtracting. It's a whole new ball game when you are multiplying or dividing . . . Good Luck!

Love, **Einstein**

Dear Einstein,

You did warn me about multiplying and dividing. I've just discovered that they are called **negative numbers** (not surprised). Guess what? I've sussed it, I don't understand or care WHY but I know it's true. This is what I say:

Signs the same, play the game:
make it PLUS

Signs are different, not the same:
make it MINUS

$$2 \times 2 = 4 \quad \textbf{but} \quad 2 \times \text{-}2 = \text{-}4$$
$$\text{-}2 \times \text{-}2 = 4 \quad \textbf{and} \quad \text{-}2 \times 2 = \text{-}4$$

The same goes for divide:

$$4 \div 2 = 2 \quad \textbf{but} \quad 4 \div \text{-}2 = \text{-}2$$
$$\text{-}4 \div \text{-}2 = 2 \quad \textbf{but} \quad 4 \div \text{-}2 = \text{-}2$$

Your ever loving, Mini-Einstein

Dear Brenda!

Worried, tired, need to understand things? **GET BETTER GRADES'** own **Agony Aunt, Brenda,** is here to answer your problems and generally make you feel a whole lot better!

Dear Brenda,

Please help me. I regularly fly a British Airlines 747 between London and Helsinki. The journey time is 2.72 hours. I take off at noon, so I always expect to arrive at 12 minutes past 3 p.m., but I always arrive at 2.43 p.m. What am I doing wrong?

Yours,

Captain A. Crash-Landing

Dear Captain A. Crash-Landing,

The mistake is a common one. **2.72 hours** is not **3 hours and 12 minutes**. What you should do is take the **2 hours** and the **0.72** separately. The **0.72 hours** converts into minutes when you multiply by **60**. So the correct answer is **2 hours and 60 x 0.72 minutes**. This makes **2 hours 43 minutes**, so you are arriving at Helsinki dead on time. I hope this makes everything a little clearer.

Yours,

Brenda

SIGNIFICANT FIGURES

Fed up with endless rows of numbers cluttering up your page?

Wish you could tidy up your digital drawer?

Now's the time for a spring clean with **GET BETTER GRADES'** own **significant figure** vacuum cleaner, the amazing Number Cruncher!

● See these rows reduce to a manageable few.

● Watch your estimations become tidy and significant.

● All you have to do is remember the **RULE OF THUMB!**

The Rule of Thumb:

"IF A NUMBER IS 5 OR MORE, YOU MUST ROUND UP THE NUMBER BEFORE IT. IF THE NUMBER IS LESS THAN 5, KEEP THE NUMBER BEFORE AS IT IS"

U S E   Y O U R   T H U M B

Say you have three numbers and you want to reduce them to **2 significant places**. Simply place your thumb over the first two numbers going from left to right and then **check out the third number**. If it is **5 or more**, simply raise the second number. If it is **less than 5**, keep the second number as it is.

Important Note:
The number that you have removed (the third one) **must** be replaced with a zero.

376 = 380

372 = 370

The rule of thumb always works, even if you have a row of **27 numbers** that you want to tidy up to just **2 significant figures**. You only need check the third number. You must remember though, always replace each number that you have removed with a **zero**.

345645689075432546765432456 =
3500000000000000000000000000 ■

Now that that's tidied up, you can start on dirty decimals. Decimals **really** tend to clutter up our significant numbers, but our super cruncher can show you how to put all those numbers after the decimal point into the digital dustbin.

IMPORTANT NOTE:

Decimals, being the rebels of the number world, **break the rule of thumb.**

DON'T DESPAIR, you can still tidy up your numbers if you remember that, after a decimal point, you use your thumb to cover up the numbers, **but don't bother to replace discarded numbers with zeros.**

If you have **three numbers** after the decimal point and you want to reduce them to **2 decimal places,** simply place your thumb over the first two numbers and then check out the third number. If it is **5 or more**, simply raise the second number. If it is **less than 5**, keep the second number as it is. Don't bother to replace the missing numbers with zeros.

7.376 = 7.38

7.372 = 7.37

THE ZERO FACTOR:

Decimals really get filthy when it comes to zeros. If you find zeros after the decimal point and before a 'real' number, **ignore them when tidying up (rounding off) to significant figures unless there is a 'real' number before the decimal point. Then, zeros must be taken into account.**

0.000048915 to two significant figures becomes **0.000049**

but

3.000048915 to two significant figures becomes **3.0**

3.06　　　　to two significant figures becomes **3.1**

3.04　　　　to two significant figures becomes **3.0**

3.98　　　　to two significant figures becomes **4.0**

Now that you have tidied up your numbers, how about starting on your bedroom??

Step into the world of the unknown,
the supernatural, the mysterious.
Welcome to the dark world of

The X Files

File 66600743: Aggravation with Algebra

Episode 1: Find the Mystery Number

Agent Muldoon skidded to a halt as the great stone door swung shut with an echoing crash. The huge figure had already passed through it into the vault, with the unconscious body of Muldoon's partner, Scullery, slung across one bandaged shoulder.

Muldoon hammered on the granite door, without effect. What was the thing that had been terrorising New York since the Egyptian Exhibition had opened? The reanimated mummy of the Pharoah Tutiphruti himself? A being from another dimension? Whatever it was, it had got Scullery. Muldoon had to get inside the vault!

Forcing himself to be calm, Muldoon examined the pattern of tiles to the right of the door. The Creature had pressed some of them to open it; but how many had it pressed and which ones?

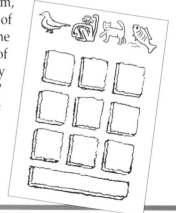

Okay. Assume the tiles were a sort of keypad, like on a calculator:

Over the tiles were four symbols carved into the rock.

The first looked like a **bird** of some kind, the second was a **monkey**, the third a **cat** (didn't the Ancient Egyptians worship cats?) and the fourth a **fish**. So the code to open the door went **bird - monkey - cat - fish.** But there were ten tiles! Muldoon decided that the long tile at the bottom was probably a zero, the next line up were the numbers **1, 2, and 3**; then **4, 5, 6**, and the top line would be **7, 8,** and **9**. That made sense; the Ancient Egyptians had practically invented maths, hadn't they? But which tiles should he press? Maybe there was a clue in the hieroglyphics above the door.

$$\text{(bird)} + 4 = 48$$

$$\text{(monkey)} - 3 = 36$$

$$\text{(cat)} \times 5 = 35$$

$$\text{(fish)} \div 2 = 24$$

Muldoon keyed in the figures after the = sign;

48363524

Nothing happened.

Too simple, thought Muldoon. Then he realised that the lines of hieroglyphics were in fact equations; he could solve them using Algebra!

Unfortunately, FBI training didn't include Algebra. Muldoon was stumped; but not for long.

Okay, he thought, try the common sense approach. Let's not call it Algebra. Let's call it 'find the mystery number'.

If he called the bird sign **'b'**, he could write the equation as
4b + 4 = 48.

If something plus **4 = 48**, that something must
be **44 (48-4)**. So **4b = 44.**
If **4 x b = 44**, then **b** must be **44 ÷ 4 = 11**.

Muldoon grinned. A bird meant 11! He was getting
somewhere!

He tried the next formula.

If **three monkeys minus 3**
came to 36, then **3m** (for 3 monkeys) **= 36 + 3 = 39.**
If **3 x m = 39**, then **m = 39 ÷ 3 = 13.**

Two down, two to go!

The next line was easy.

If a cat **(c)** multiplied by **5 = 35,**
then **c = 35 ÷ 5 = 7.**

The final line; if **f ÷ 2 = 24,**
then **f = 2 x 24 = 48.**

Holding his breath, Muldoon keyed
in the new numbers;

1 1 1 3 7 4 8

The great stone door ground
slowly open. Once more, Muldoon
prepared to enter the world
of the Unknown.......

For the next thrilling episode of The X Files, turn to p **42**

Dear Brenda!

Dear Brenda,

This guy from the Inland Revenue comes snooping round my place. He wants to know why I have not filled in any tax returns for the past 15 years, also what is the gross amount I make every year out of illegal gambling, protection rackets and hustling generally. He also reckons I might be liable for VAT.

My question is this. If it takes 8 guys with 4 wheelbarrows 9 days to shift 27 cubic metres of cement, how long will it take 4 guys with 2 wheelbarrows to bury this nosy stiff under a bridge support on the M 25?

Dodgy Nick

Dear Dodgy Nick,

I certainly have no intention of helping you dispose of the bodies of tax inspectors.

However, for an answer to your mathematical conundrum, you need to look at the section on **scale factors** (p 52). All these questions about water filling baths and men building walls (and gangsters burying stiffs) are the same, but examiners keep trying to find new ways of setting them so you'll be tricked into thinking this is a problem you haven't come across before. Don't be fooled!

Anyway, Nick, I advise you to hire a good crooked accountant; this won't only bring your tax bill down, it'll save you a fortune in cement.

Love,

Brenda

SHAPE UP FOR SUMMER!

Shape up with the following shapes

Just some of the shapes you'll be meeting up with in the exam hall.

PUMP IT UP!

Get into the gym and tone up your quadrilaterals for a stunning figure in your exams!

A quadrilateral is a 4-sided shape. Inside every quadrilateral are four angles. These angles add up to 360°.

SQUARE

- A 4-sided figure.
- All sides are equal length.
- All angles are right angles
- There are 4 lines of symmetry.
- Rotational symmetry order 4.

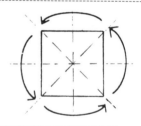

RECTANGLE (or oblong)

- A 4-sided figure with opposite sides which are equal in length.
- All angles are right angles.
- Its diagonals are equal in length.
- It has 2 lines of symmetry.
- Rotational symmetry order 2.

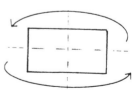

RHOMBUS (sometimes called a diamond)
- A 4-sided figure with all sides of equal length.
- 2 of these sides are parallel.
- The diagonals bisect each other at right angles.
- It has 2 lines of symmetry.
- Rotational symmetry order 2.

PARALLELOGRAM
- A 4-sided figure with opposite sides
  equal in length and parallel to each other.
- 2 angles diagonally opposite each other are equal.
- It has NO lines of symmetry.
- Rotational symmetry order 2.

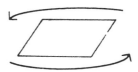

KITE
- A 4-sided shape made up of
  2 isosceles triangles with the same base.
- 1 line of symmetry.
- No rotational symmetry.

TRAPEZIUM
- A 4-sided shape with only 2 sides parallel.
- A bit like a triangle with its top cut off!
- Only an isosceles trapezium has a line of symmetry.
- No trapezium has rotational symmetry.

 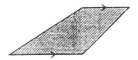

THE TRIANGLE PROGRAMME

You too can have a triangle figure like mine!

Types of Triangles

A triangle is a polygon with 3 sides.
The 3 angles in a triangle add up to 180°.
There are several types of triangle.

A SCALENE TRIANGLE
• A figure with all 3 sides having different lengths and 3 different angles.

AN ISOSCELES TRIANGLE
• A 3-sided figure with two sides of equal length and having 2 of its angles equal.
• 1 line of symmetry.
• No rotational symmetry.

AN EQUILATERAL TRIANGLE
• A figure with all 3 sides equal in length and all three angles the same.
• It has 3 lines of symmetry.
• Rotational symmetry order 3.

A RIGHT-ANGLED TRIANGLE
• A 3-sided figure with 1 of its angles being 90°.
• It has no line of symmetry, unless the angles are 45°.

SOLID MUSCLE

Get really solid and know the names of these:

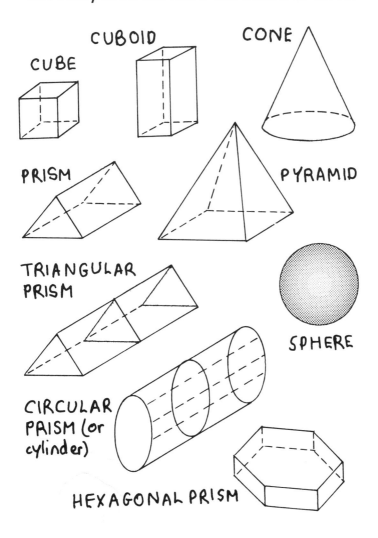

CUBE

CUBOID

CONE

PRISM

PYRAMID

TRIANGULAR PRISM

SPHERE

CIRCULAR PRISM (or cylinder)

HEXAGONAL PRISM

a) A dead parrot

b) A missing parrot

c) A many-sided shape

d) The name of a Bulgarian shotputter

Answer: Oh come on! Surely we don't have to tell you!

A regular polygon has:

- the same number of sides and equal angles.
- the same number of lines of symmetry as it has sides.
- the same order of rotational symmetry as it has sides.

FOREIGN BIT

The names for polygons are based on Greek and Roman words for numbers.
For instance **dec** is Latin for 10.
Therefore a **decagon** is a shape with ten sides.

Polygon names

Number of sides	Name
3	triangle
4	quadrilateral
5	pentagon
6	hexagon
7	heptagon
8	octagon
9	nonagon
10	decagon
12	dodecagon

SOME MORE REGULAR POLYGONS

PENTAGON

- 5 sides
- 5 lines of symmetry
- Rotational symmetry order 5

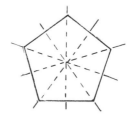

HEXAGON

- 6 sides
- 6 lines of symmetry
- Rotational symmetry order 6

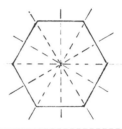

HEPTAGON

- 7 sides
- 7 lines of symmetry
- Rotational symmetry order 7

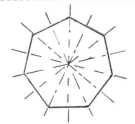

OCTAGON

- 8 sides
- 8 lines of symmetry
- Rotational symmetry order 8

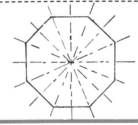

Episode 2: Trial and Terror

When Muldoon burst into the inner chamber, he found Scullery lying helpless on a slab of rock which was balanced on top of a narrow ridge. Muldoon gasped in horror. If the slab tilted one way, Scullery would be tipped into a bottomless pit; if it tilted the other, she would slide into a pit full of deadly scorpions!

In front of him was a small platform of the sort you find on weighing machines, and several stones all the same size, which looked like weights.

Scullery raised her head. She knew she couldn't move, and Muldoon couldn't reach her.

Muldoon realised there was another equation written on the side of the slab. It read...

$$\text{🦆🦆🦆} + 15 = 39 - \text{🦆🦆🦆🦆🦆}$$

(3 pelicans) + 15 = 39 - (5 pelicans)

Or, to put it another way, **3p + 15 = 39 - 5p.**

"There's some sort of equation here," Muldoon told Scullery, "but it's tough. The pelican means an unknown number, but it's on both sides of the equation, so how can I work it out?"

"You'll have to try guessing," called Scullery, "but for Pete's sake be careful!"

Suppose, thought Muldoon, a pelican **(p)** is worth 1.

He put one stone on the platform.

The slab started to slide towards the bottomless pit! Scullery scrabbled desperately. Muldoon substituted numbers furiously. He got:

If p = 1, 3 + 15 = 39 - 5, 18 = 34

The sides didn't balance! The figure on the right was too big. No wonder the slab was tipping!

Hastily, Muldoon removed the stone. The slab reluctantly rocked back to a level position.

"Muldoon," hissed Scullery, "I hope you know what you're doing!"

So do I, thought Muldoon. OK, suppose **p=5.**

He dropped five weights onto the platform.

This time, the slab tilted towards the scorpions. Too much! Muldoon swept the weights aside.

"Muldoon, will you quit fooling around!"

Muldoon checked his figures.

If p = 5, then 15 + 15 = 39 - 25,   30 = 14

This time, the figure on the left was too big. **p** must be something in between **1 and 5**. This time, Muldoon decided to work out the equation before he tried putting weights on the platform.

Suppose p = 3, then 9 + 15 = 39 - 15, 24 = 24

Yes! This time, the figures balanced. Muldoon put three weights on the platform. The slab swivelled round, and Scullery scrambled to safety!

To find his answer, Muldoon used the **trial and error** (sometimes called the **trial and improvement**) **method**. Usually a question will give you examples of how to do your working. All you have to do is keep trying until you get the right answer.

For the final episode of The X Files, turn to page **85**

Titus Lines our fishing expert, helps you out with a few angling tips. **Angling for marks is easy in exams if you know the rules and top tips for catching that whopper of a grade.**

FIRST OF ALL - KNOW YOUR ANGLES

This can give you a head start if you know what sort of angle you are dealing with.

Angles are measured by how much of a turn they represent.

Full turn	$= 360°$
Straight line (half a turn)	$= 180°$
Right angle (quarter of a turn)	$= 90°$

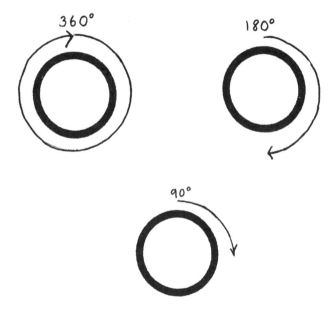

AN ACUTE ANGLE

Look at the lines on this little gem. It's good to look at, cute in fact, but there's not much eating on this - not much body on it at all. Lovely small body - tight, less than 90°.

AN OBTUSE ANGLE

Now this has got a good body on it. Plenty of meat and we can tell that it measures more than 90° but less than 180°.

A REFLEX ANGLE

This is a real whopper! It's easy to spot as it's so big.

If you see an angle like this you know it's going to be more than 180°.

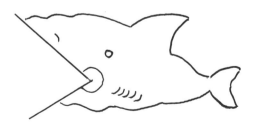

Now follow these rules of angling to help you pull in that top mark.

1. The angles in a triangle add up to **180°**
2. The angles in a quadrilateral add up to **360°**
3. The angles round a point add up to **360°**
4. The angles on a straight line add up to **180°**
5. Whenever one line crosses two parallel lines the angles are going to be **the same** at the point of crossing.
6. In an isosceles triangle, you need only know one angle to be able to work out the other two.

If you get stuck with an angling problem, try out all of the above rules.

We all know that we need to measure the fish we catch - we can measure angles as well, by using a protractor.

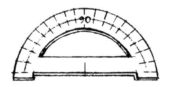

Don't use the wrong side - you might end up exaggerating your angle and of course we know that good fishermen (and women) never exaggerate!

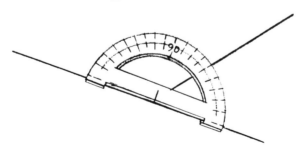

Here we have measurement of **130°**.

We know it can't be 50°, because it is an obtuse angle (i.e. between 90° and 180).

Best to estimate an angle, then measure it - we don't want to let people think that we don't get our measurements right!

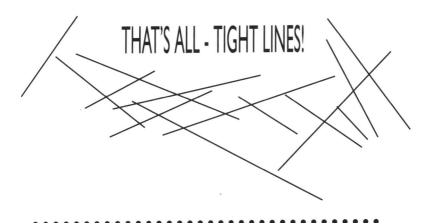

THAT'S ALL - TIGHT LINES!

• •

ABACUS

A calculating device consisting of balls strung on wires or rods set in a frame. It is probably of Babylonian origin but its use declined in Europe with the introduction of Arabic numerals in about the 10th century AD. Until recently it was still in use in the Middle East and Japan.

GREAT MATHEMATICAL COCKUPS OF THE PAST

Isembard Kingdom Wilkinson was one of the greatest designers of Victorian England. Sadly, his name is now all but forgotten.

Like his namesake, Brunel, Wilkinson could turn his hand to designing anything; bridges, railway engines, factories. Brunel, of course, went on to build such staggering monuments to Victorian ingenuity as the Clifton Suspension Bridge, the Menai Bridge and the first iron-hulled steamships such as the *Great Eastern*.

In contrast, Wilkinson never built anything that worked properly without collapsing, sinking or blowing up. He sank into drunkenness and despair, and died, a broken man, before his thirtieth year.

In his tragically short (but, tragically, not short enough) lifetime, Wilkinson had built factories smaller than dog kennels; railway bridges three miles long and fifteen centimetres wide; and boilers fifteen metres in diameter which, when he tried to fit them into ships less than four metres in length, immediately sank the vessels they were intended to power.

The reason for this was very simple: **Wilkinson simply did not understand how to use scale!**

On one notorious occasion, the builders of one of Wilkinson's bridges were trying to interpret a drawing:

As the scale given on the plan was **1 : 5**, the builders assumed that since the bridge on the plan was **1m wide**, the actual bridge was designed to be **5m** wide.

In fact, Wilkinson had forgotten to record the small but important fact that the scale he meant to use was **1cm : 5m**, which he should have written as

1 : 500.

So, the **500 metre bridge** that Wilkinson had designed to carry the railway over the mighty River Thames ended up as an ornamental feature over the boating lake in a municipal park at Leighton Buzzard.

Another time, he was asked to build a great iron tower at Bognor Regis to rival the one at Blackpool. This time, Wilkinson got somebody else to draw the plans for him at a scale of **1cm : 100cm**.

Unfortunately, Wilkinson got things the wrong way round. He assumed that, since the tower in the drawing was

175 cms high, its ACTUAL height was

175 ÷ 100 = 1.75 centimetres.

He was wrong.

The **first** figure in a scale on a **plan** refers to the **size of the drawing.**

The second figure refers to the **actual size**.

Wilkinson got these figures reversed.

He should, of course, have multiplied the scale figure by 100:

175 cm on the plan =
175 x 100 = 17500 cm
or 175 metres

At 175 metres, the Bognor Tower would have been comfortably bigger than the Blackpool Tower and brought fame and fortune to West Sussex. The tower Wilkinson built was, in fact, under 2 centimetres tall. The Wilkinson family kept it in a drawer for 90 years. Eventually it was sold at an auction, described as a 'novelty paper weight'.

ENLARGEMENTS

Of course, a scale of 1 : 1 would be easiest to use, but it's not always practical. If you're designing a Boeing 747, you really wouldn't want to have to use a piece of paper as big as the aeroplane itself!

SCALE FACTOR

Sometimes, the **SCALE FACTOR** is given as a single figure (eg **2.5)** rather than a ratio (eg **1:50)**.

TOP TIP

If the **SCALE FACTOR** is **bigger** than 1, the shape you are enlarging gets **bigger**.

If the **SCALE FACTOR** is **smaller** than 1, the shape you are enlarging gets **smaller**. (This is really a reduction, but for some reason best known to mathematicians, it's still called an ENLARGEMENT. Hey ho.)

You can find out the **SCALE FACTOR** by using this **Absolutely Brill** formula triangle:

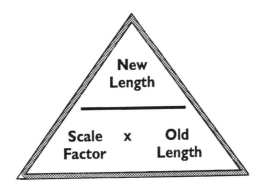

SHOW BIZ GOSSIP WITH BARBARELLA JOCKSTRAP

The word on the street is that Baz O'Dosh, the famous Irish rock singer, has bought a brand new helicopter, so his old helipad is too small. All together now, 'Aaaaaah!'

When the builders got the plans for the new helipad. . . they discovered that the plan had one measurement missing.

No problem, the builders knew that both helipads were **similar**; that is, they were the same shape, but different sizes; so they could use the Formula Triangle to work out the length of the missing side.

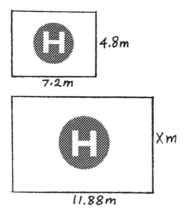

Step 1: To find the Scale Factor:
Scale Factor = New Length ÷ Old Length = 11.88 ÷ 7.2 = 1.65
Step 2: To find the New Width (x m)
New Width = Scale Factor x Old Width = 1.65 x 4.8 = 7.92 m

But was a new helipad enough for our Baz? No way Jose!
Baz decided to build a hanger for his helicopter using the Scale Factor. Sad-lee, the finished hangar was barely big enough to garage his Porsche. This was because Baz had never read **Barbarella's Factorizing** TOP TIP ?!

Remember you can only use the **Scale Factor** to work out lengths and widths.

To work out area, you need the **(Scale Factor)^2**

To work out volume, you need the **(Scale Factor)^3**

i.e. if the **Scale Factor** is 3; the lengths are 3 times as big, each area is 3 x 3 = 9 times as big,

and each volume is 3 x 3 x 3 = 27 times as big!

So poor Baz's helicopter has to stand out in the rain. **THAT'S SHOWBIZ, BAZ**!

You can also use this method to work out photographic enlargements (a fave exam question, this).

Arab mathematicians invented the number 0 ('zero') which the Romans didn't have, and also separate symbols for each number.

The term 'algebra' comes from Mohammed ibn Musa Al-Khowarizmi's book *Al habra w'al muqabalah*.

Get Better Grades Short Story time

RATIO, RATIO!

CHAPTER 1
Red-faced

When Jason and Debbie were sentenced to community service (never mind what for, they don't want to talk about it), they were sent to paint a club.

"It's a Yoof club," the project leader had explained. "For Yoof," he had added, in case they'd missed the point.

So here they were in a place the size of a barn with **10 one-litre** cans of red paint and **10 one-litre** cans of white paint, two buckets, two rollers and a paint chart. The project leader had marked the shade of pink he wanted on the chart.

"It says mix red and white in a ratio of 4 : 8," said Jason. "Wossat mean?"

"Well," said Debbie, who had paid more attention in school maths lessons, "it means that for every **4 tins** of red paint, you need to mix in **eight tins** of white."

Jason added up on his fingers. "**4 plus 8, that's 12 litres**. Them buckets'll never hold 12 litres, that's more than two gallons." Jason wasn't too hot on maths, but he was well-up on petrol conversion tables and cars in general, which was something to do with how he ended up doing community service.

_____

"Right," said Debbie, "but you don't need to use **12 litres** of paint."

"But you said..."

"I said for every **4 tins of red** you'd need **8 white**, but suppose you only used **1 tin of red**?"

"You'd get the wrong colour?"

Debbie sighed. "Not if you divided both sides of the ratio

by the same amount." She scribbled on a wall in pencil;

4 : 8 = (4÷4) : (8 ÷ 4) = 1 : 2

"You'll have to wash that off."

"We're going to paint over it, div."

Jason looked hurt. "Anyway, why **divide by 4**?"

"Because it works. When you work out ratios, you just have to simplify if you can to make the maths easier."

"Hey," Jason suddenly brightened, "like racing odds! You know, if a horse is backed at **20 : 1**, and the odds shorten, you don't call it **20 : 2**, you call it **10 : 1**."

Debbie stared at him. "So you do understand about ratios."

Jason was scornful. "That's not ratios. That's odds."

"Same thing. Anyway, let's mix **one tin of red** to **two of white** and get started."

TOP TIP
You can write a **RATIO** as a **FRACTION** or a **DECIMAL**:

eg 5 : 10 = 1 / 2 = 5 : 10 = 0.5

If your calculator has a **FRACTION BUTTON**, you can use that:

i.e. to simplify **5 : 10**, key in **5 (fraction button) 10 (equals button)**

The answer will be ½, which means the same as the ratio **1 : 2**.

But be careful! The fraction button only works on whole numbers, so if you start off with fractions, you have to convert them into whole numbers first.

Both Jason and Debbie made up a mix of one tin of red and two of white. They were just finishing the last wall when the project leader bounded in. "Change of plan," he gasped. "The committee don't like the colour, they want a deeper pink. More reddy. This one." He pointed at a different colour on the chart.

"**Ratio of 5 : 8**," read Debbie. "But we used **four tins of**

white on the first lot, we've only got **six tins** left."

"You'll just have to work it out, I'm afraid." The project director bounded off to ruin someone else's day.

Jason stared at the tins. "Five into eight won't go."

"Nope. Time for a formula triangle. Check this out."

On the last bit of unpainted wall, Debbie scribbled:

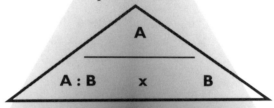

Jason screwed his eyes up. "What's that supposed to mean?"

"A is the first figure in the ratio, B is the second. The ratio is 5 : 8 and we want to know how many cans of red paint we have to mix with 6 cans of white, right?"

"White. I mean, right."

"So we write it as:

$$\frac{\text{red}}{5:8 \quad x \quad 6} \text{ (white cans)}$$

"Now, we have to make the ratio into a fraction so we can do the calculation. $5 : 8 = \frac{5}{8}$ so we have:

$$\text{red cans} = \frac{5 \times 6}{8} = \frac{30}{8} = 3\frac{6}{8}$$

"In other words, if we mix three and three quarters cans of red with the six cans of white we have left, we should get the right colour."

Jason scowled. "And then HE'LL come along and want to change the colour again. Betcha."

"What odds?"

"**6 : 4**."

"You're on."

RATIO! RATIO!

CHAPTER 2

The Sum of the PARTS

Later on, Jason and Debbie were joined by Jen, and they all decided to form a Lottery syndicate. They agreed that they'd divide any winnings according to the amount they put in. The first week:

Jason put in **£3**, Debbie put in **£8** and Jen put in **£5**.

They got lucky! They won **£2,400** between them.

When the time came to divvy this out, they were stumped, until Debbie remembered about **PARTS**.

She wrote out the amounts they'd all put in as a ratio:

i.e. 3 : 8 : 5.

Get Better Grades   TOP TIP

When you have to do Proportional Division:

FIRST, add up all the **parts.**

SECOND, find **ONE part** by dividing the total to be divided by the number of parts.

THIRD, multiply **one part by each share**; there's your answer.

Debbie worked it out: **3 + 8 + 5 = 16**
One part = £2400 ÷ 16 = £150

So: Jason got **3 x 150 = £450**

Debbie got   **8 x 150 = £1200**

Jen got   **5 x 150 = £750**

And did the other two feel jealous of Debbie?   Mebbe!

What is power?

Well in maths **7 to the power of 3** is 7^3 and means **7 x 7 x 7** which is equal to **343.** Now this could be the case for any number. **23 to the power 2** is 23^2 = **23 x 23** or letter in algebra,

y to the power 3 is y^3 = y x y x y

n to the power 2 is n^2 = n x n.

This can be extended to any number for the **power 4^6** = 4 x 4 x 4 x 4 x 4 x 4 and so on.

3^2 is usually called 3 squared.

4^3 is usually called 4 cubed.

There are several rules to do with powers
$$4^3 \text{ x } 4^5 = 4^8$$
When multiplying powers of the same number you can **add** both the powers.

The bottom number must always be the same.

When dividing powers of the same number
$$7^6 \div 7^3 = 7^{6-3} = 7^3$$
you can **subtract** powers.

POWERS

Rule $9^1 = 9$

If there is no power written on a number it is always to the power of 1.

Rule $2° = 1$, $10° = 1$, $23984° = 1$

If you want to raise 4^3 to the **power 5**, you would write it as $(4^3)^5$ but this is $4^3 \times 4 \times 4 \times 4 \times 4 \times 4$ so if you use the rule for adding powers this becomes 4^{15}. You could have done this just as easily by working out $4^{3+5} = 4^{15}$.

One last rule: $5^{-1} = \frac{1}{5}$.

THE ROOT
OF ALL EVIL

What does $\sqrt{\ }$ (square root) mean?

Well, $3^2 = 9$ $\sqrt{9} = 3$.   It's the opposite of squared. Most calculators have this button so you just type in the number and press the button.

You use this when you want to solve an equation like $x^2 = 16$.

Think about Pythagoras' theorem (see page 73).
You need to use it.
There are other roots like $\sqrt[3]{\ }$
This is the opposite of cubed. $4^3 = 4 \times 4 \times 4 = 64^3$ $\sqrt[3]{64} = 4$

If you want to write $\sqrt{9}$ as a power you write $9^{1/2}$

SPOT THE DIFFERENCE

Can you spot the difference between these numbers?

a) 5.5 x 10 x 10 x 10 x 10

b) 5.5 x 10^4

c) 55,000

THAT'S RIGHT, there isn't a difference!
They are simply different ways of writing them down.
5.5 x 10^4 is called **standard form.**
55,000 is called **ordinary number.**

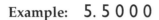 **STANDARD FORM** is a quick way of writing down numbers with lots of zeros in.

n is the number of places, the decimal point moves.

$$a \times 10^n$$

a is a number between 1 and 9.

Example: 5. 5 0 0 0

The decimal point moves 4 places, so it is written:

$$5.5 \times 10^4$$

(**Remember** 5.5 is a number between 1 and 9.)

USING A CALCULATOR

Scientific calculators will show large numbers in standard form.

Reading a standard form number from the display:

If you wished to find out the answer to **40000 x 40000,** enter **40000 x 40000** into the calculator.
The answer will then be displayed like this:

This is a calculator's
way of writing **1.6 x 10⁹**
(As an ordinary number
it would be written:
1 600 000 000)

Entering a standard form number into the calculator:

If you wanted to enter **1.6 x 10⁹**

Press 1.6 EXP (or EE) 9

ANOTHER SPOT THE DIFFERENCE
What is the difference between the following?
a) Standard Form
b) Standard Index Form

Again, there is **NO** difference.
Standard Form and **Standard Index Form** are the same thing!

EXAM QUESTION

Express 321000 in standard form

THE ANSWER

1) Move the decimal point until **321000** becomes a number between **1** and **10** ie **3.21**

2) Count how many places the **decimal point** has moved.

$$3.\overset{\frown}{2}\,\overset{\frown}{1}\,\overset{\frown}{0}\,\overset{\frown}{0}\,\overset{\frown}{0}\,0. = 5$$

Therefore **321,000** in **standard form** is written 3.21×10^5

Standard form can be used to show small numbers as well.

0.0000321 can be written:

3.21×10^{-5}

Because **n** is negative, it means that the number is going to be less than 1.

EXAMPLE
Express 5.5×10^{-5} as an ordinary number.

THE ANSWER
$^{-5}$ tells us that a is going to be less than **1 (a small number)**
10^{-5} tells us that the **decimal point** has to move **5 spaces**

So $0.\overset{\frown}{0}\,\overset{\frown}{0}\,\overset{\frown}{0}\,\overset{\frown}{0}\,\overset{\frown}{5}.5$

The Magic Circle

David Copperbottom and his glamorous assistant, Cherry Pi, welcome you into the world of the Circle Magique.

Here's your chance to join one of the most exclusive clubs in the world. Amaze your friends, astound your teachers, and you might even Get Better Grades as you unlock the secrets of the sinister circle and gain entry to the mysteries of the world of **Pi**.

As with any club, there are certain rituals and incantations to learn. Don't worry; there are very few things to remember and, once you have learned the appropriate tricks, the magic circle will hold no mysteries for you.

Equipment necessary:

1. Inflatable rabbit (optional).

2. Scientific calculator.

3. Compass (no, not the one with the magnetic needle).

4. Protractor.

5. A really sincere smile.

The password for unlocking the secrets of the circle is π, the sixteenth letter of the Greek alphabet (isn't that fascinating?) and pronounced, and sometimes written, as **Pi**.

This letter has mystical properties to it and should be used only when you are dealing with the **Magic Circle**. If ever you try to use **Pi** to gain entry to any other club (the ridiculous **Rhombus** or the twisted **Trapezoids**), you will be thrown out of the **Magic Circle**, and your obvious hairpiece will be ritually torched.

The numerologists have given π a value of **3.14.** . . . . Those extra dots are not a printing error. They indicate that π goes on for ever - that's how mystical the number is. In fact, you could write the value of π from here to Mars and not come to the final number - try it! Now that a couple of nerds are writing down the value of π, the rest of us can get on with the initiation rights of the **Magic Circle**.

To be a really successful member, you have to understand a couple of club rules, and to know the few words of the club's special language.

1. Circle:

A plain figure in which all points on the surrounding edge are equidistant from a fixed point. (Don't bother memorising this definition because any fool knows what a circle is.)

2. Circumference:

The edge of a circle, going all the way around.

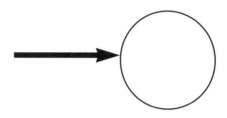

3. Diameter, known to **Magic Circle** members as **'D'**:
A straight line touching two parts of the
circumference, and passing through the
centre of the circle.

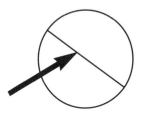

4. Radius, known to **Magic Circle** members as **'R'**:
A straight line going from the centre of the circle to a
point on its circumference.

Interesting thought:
As the plural of radius is radii, is the plural of yo yo, yo yi?

Now that you know the club's language, you can start to
learn a few tricks. If you wanted to reveal the length of the
circumference of a circle, you could walk around it (difficult
to do if you wanted to find out the circumference of a 10p
coin), you could measure it (got a really flexible ruler?).
Now, the diameter is easy to measure because it's a straight
line, so you could use this measurement and the club's
password π.

Circumference = π x Diameter = πD

Here is a circle to try it on:

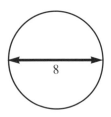

Step one: Stop playing with the inflatable rabbit.

Step two: Measure the diameter. Actually, we've done that and you can see that the diameter is eight.

Step three: Turn the calculator on, press the π button, press the x button, and then press 8. The answer is **25.13,** and that is the circumference.

To find out the area of a circle, you could fill it with tiny squares and count the squares, except, of course, some of the squares would be cut off at the circumference of the circle, and why are we even suggesting such a stupid method? The easy solution is at hand in The Magic Circle. Simply learn the incantation:

AREA = π x Radius squared = π R²

Step one: Straighten your hairpiece.

Step two: Measure the radius. Yes, yes, we've done that for you too and you can see that it's 4. Hey, could it be that the radius is half the diameter? Check it out!!

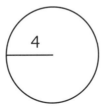

Step three: Turn the calculator on, press the π button, press the x button, press 4 and then the x^2 button. Your answer should be close to **50.265**. If it is, you now qualify for membership to the **Magic Circle**.

I heard that, and yes, it is a big deal if you want to **Get Better Grades!**

Two more terms to make you feel at ease in the **Magic Circle:**

Tangent: Something to divert your maths teacher so he/she goes off on one or a straight line that just touches the edge of a circle. When it meets the radius, they make an angle of 90 degrees.

Chord: Yes, we resisted references to banjos, and are telling you that it is simply a line that goes across a circle, and has each end touching the circumference. If a chord meets a line at 90 degrees and that line divides the chord in half, that line will be a diameter. (Why should radii have all the fun?)

Fascinating (honest!) fact:

If you draw a triangle from both ends of the diameter, the angle that the lines form when they touch the circumference will automatically be 90 degrees - WOW!

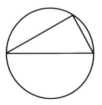

THINGS YOU MAY NOT KNOW ABOUT PYTHAGORAS

(The man with the famous theorem)

- He was born around the year 582 BC and died some 85 years later. (Some students wish he'd died a lot sooner - then they wouldn't have had to bother with his theorem.)

- Although he was born in Greece, he lived in Italy for most of his life.

- He was more interested in religion than mathematics, and was known as a famous mystic and religious leader.

- He ruled the religious community he lived in - his followers had to obey his way of life, called Pythagoreanism.

I'M SORRY I CAN ONLY DO MATHS IN THE SUMMER, AS IT'S BAD FOR MY HEALTH!

- One of his rules was that no one should eat beans as he believed in reincarnation and thought that people could come back as beans! Human Beans? - ho ho!

- He also had strange ideas about sex. He said you should only make love in the summer, not the winter, as it was bad for the health.

• Pythagoras believed some numbers were magical and based much of his mathematical work on Egyptian magic!
• He also made discoveries about musical notes and the mathematical relationship between musical intervals.
• His followers worshipped the magical equilateral triangle of 10 dots.
• He is known nowadays for his theorem concerning triangles.

HOW TO CREEP TO YOUR MATHS TEACHER

If you are asked by your maths teacher what you think of their lessons, say "Maths is magic!" The teacher will think that you mean that the lessons are good, but what you're really saying is that they're based on magic! This will get you in their good books and you'll probably get a Grade A! *

*But then again...

It's all Greek to us!

Pythagoras' theorem. What is it? Let Pythagoras explain:

I hope that makes it all clear!

Publishers Memo

What do you think you're playing at! How many Greek readers do you think we have? Even I don't understand this and I'm a real brainbox intellectual!

Sort this out IMMEDIATELY or else there's no money for you!

The publisher

Dear Margie, Lee, Owen + Steve,
Looks as if the publisher has called our bluff - we're going to have to explain all that stuff about the loony Greek guy. Otherwise we don't get any money.
Steve

Dear Steve,
Damn!
Owen Lee
Steve
Margie

Okay.........

What's it all about?

Pythagoras' theorem is used to work out the length of the third side of a right angled triangle, when the other two sides' lengths are known.

If you draw a square on the longest side of a right angled triangle, its area is equal to the sum of the squares drawn on the two shorter sides.

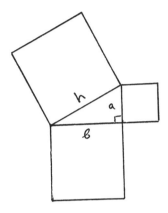

THE FORMULA

$$h^2 = a^2 + b^2$$

or put another way

$$a^2 + b^2 = h^2$$

Do not confuse a hypotenuse with a hippopotamus.

How to tell them apart:

It should be fairly easy to tell which is which.

HOW TO CHEAT WITHOUT CHEATING

• Square the two numbers that you are given on the calculator by using the

$$x^2 \text{ button}$$

• Add or subtract:

To find the longest side ADD these two squared numbers.

To find a shorter side, SUBTRACT the smaller number from the larger.

• Square root:

The next step is to find the square root of the answer you have just got by

pressing the $\sqrt{}$ button

• Check:

Is the answer a sensible one ?

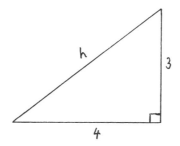

How to work h out easily!

- SQUARE:

$4^2 = 16$

$3^2 = 9$

We wish to find the longest side so:

- ADD:

$16 + 9 = 25$

- SQUARE ROOT:

$\sqrt{25} = 5$

- CHECK:

5 is longer than than 4 and 3 but not excessively so. This seems about right.

QUICK CALCULATOR SEQUENCE

(scientific calculator with BODMAS)

Use this method for speedy calculator results.

PUSH BUTTON	WHAT YOU WILL SEE	
4	4	
x^2	16	
+	16	
3	3	
x^2	9	
=	25	
$\sqrt{}$	5	the answer

THAT'S BETTER!
Publisher

Dear Publisher
So where's our money?
The team

Dear ALL
Ah, er, funny you
should mention
that................

SPOT THE DIFFERENCE

A ☐   B ☐

Can you spot the difference?

No? Well there is. Square B is upside down! But there's still no difference you say!

Well, yes. That's because a square has a line of symmetry. It has mirror lines. This means that if you folded the drawing in half along a mirror line, the two halves would meet up EXACTLY (i.e. one half would be a reflection of the other).

Dear Brenda,
  Is there a quick way of working out how many lines of symmetry a shape has?
  Your mirrored and confused
    Snow White

Dear Snow White,
Yes there is!
  All regular polygons have the same number of lines of symmetry as sides.
  See also page 42
  Yours,
    Brenda

You might want to use a mirror to see if a drawing / shape has line symmetry. Simply place the mirror on the mirror line and look at the reflection. Does it match the shape exactly.

Rotational symmetry

The order of rotational symmetry is the number of times a shape will fit into its original shape in one full rotation.

A square fits into itself 4 times.

The letter H has a rotational symmetry order 2, because it fits into its own shape twice.

eg

Original position   **H**

Half turn   **H⌡**

Original position   **⌠H⌡**

TOP TIP

All shapes fit into their own shape! Examiners may be feeling mean and not count this. So if you're asked if a shape has a rotational symmetry and it only fits into its own shape, say NO!

Dear Brenda

I'm feeling lazy again! Is there a quick way of working out how many orders of rotational symmetry a shape has?

Yours still mirrored and confused.

Snow White

Dear Snow White

Yes there is!

All **regular** polygons have the same order of rotational symmetry as sides.

Brenda

PS

A warning to you. Avoid small men and old women with apples.

BE A HERO!

You are in the control room of the world renowned disaster troubleshooters, RESCUES 'R' WE. There are several disasters that need the help of the RESCUES 'R' WE computerised flying machine.

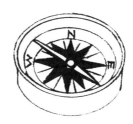

What you have to do is simply work out the bearing that the Rescue Machine will need to take to reach each of the disasters.

HINTS TO HELP

• A bearing is the direction travelled between two points
• They are given as angles measured from the North line in a clockwise direction.
• Draw in a North line from the starting point.
• Measure the angle with a protractor.
• All bearings should be given as 3 figures
i.e. 270°, 090° (not 90°) 005° (not 5°).

Eg. Find the bearing from A to B.

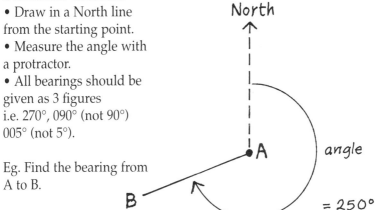

What bearing does the RESCUES 'R' WE helicopter need to take to:

1) Rescue the woman from the clutches of the big monkey?
2) Stop the mad professor from blowing up an atomic bomb?
3) Stop the QE II from sinking?
4) Stop the Leaning Tower of Pisa from falling over?
5) Stop the jumbo jet landing on a city?
6) Rescue the puppy dog from drowning?

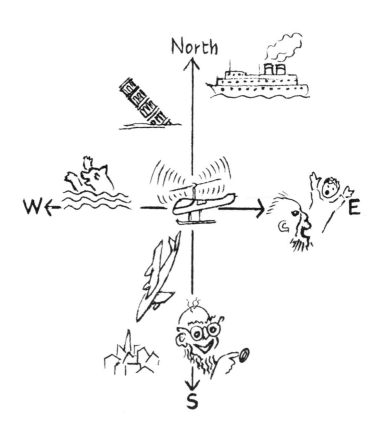

Answers 1) 090° 2) 180° 3) 010° 4) 345° 5) 200° 6) 270°

Percy Guzzard's DIY tips

Better Grades' own Do-It-Yourself expert, Percy Guzzard, gives you his tips on how to work out the area of essential shapes you might come up against when you want to wallpaper a house!*

First off all you need a wall! These come in all sorts of shapes and sizes, so you'll need to know what shape your wall is! (see page 36).

Then we need to find out the area. Why? Because you have to know how much wallpaper you need. There's nothing more annoying than running out of wallpaper when you're up to your eyeballs in paste and paper, because you haven't worked out the wall's area.

And it's so simple! Even my apprentice, Gormless Gordon, can work it out.

For rectangular and square shaped walls: you'll need to know the length and the width of the rectangle (or square). Then simple multiply the length by the width. This will give you the area (which will always be in squared units) eg:

Rectangle & Square

Area = L x W

$5 \text{ m} \times 3 \text{ m} = 15 \text{ m}^2$

3

5

* Or work out areas in a maths exam.

For tricky shapes you'll have to use the following formulae

Triangle

Area of triangle = $\frac{1}{2}$ x Base x Vertical Height

A = $\frac{1}{2}$ x B x Hv

$\frac{1}{2}$ x 5 x 3 = 7.5 m^2

Remember that this has to be the vertical height, not the sloping height.

If you have walls shaped like this you ought to think about moving as your house will probably be collapsing very soon!

Parallelogram

Area of parallelogram = Base x Vertical Height

A = B x Hv

5 m x 3 m = 15 m^2

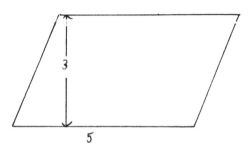

Trapezium

Area of trapezium = average of parallel sides x distance between them (the height).

A = ½ x (a+b) x H

½ x (5m + 4m) x 3m = A

½ x 9m x 3m = 13.5 m^2

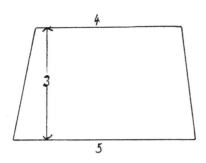

Oldest mathematical puzzle

'As I was going to St. Ives,
I met a man with seven wives.
Every wife had seven sacks,
and every sack had seven cats.
Every cat had seven kits.
Kits, cats, sacks and wives,
How many were going to St. Ives?'

Apart from slight differences in wording, this is identical to a puzzle found in the Rhind papyrus, an Egyptian scroll bearing mathematical tables and problems, copied by the scribe Ahmes c. 1650 BC.

P.S. Answer 1!!

When I need to fill up buckets with paint and water (and my mug with tea and pint pot with beer), or my sandwich box with my favourite fish paste sandwiches, I need to know all about VOLUMES.Volume is the amount of space a three dimensional shape takes up! It is measured in cubes.

Cuboid

(Also known as a rectangular block and the same shape as my lunchbox.)

Volume of cuboid = Length x Width x Height

V= L x W x H

5m x 4m x 3m = 60 m^3

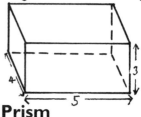

Prism

A prism is a solid object which has a constant area of cross section (it is the same shape all the way through)

BETTER GRADES

You have to find the cross-sectional area first. This is the hardest part of finding the volume of a prism.

Volume of prism = Cross-sectional Area x Length

V = A x L

Step 1: Find the cross-sectional area. To find area of the above circle, use the Magic Circle formulae (see page 63).

A = π x R^2

3.14 x 25cm = 78.5cm^2

Step 2: Use V = A x L

78.5cm^2 x 20 cm = 1570 cm^3

The X Files

Episode 3: The Bracket Racket

Muldoon and Scullery burst through the doorway into the innermost sanctum. The Creature stood before them.

Scullery clenched her fists. "Who are you? What do you want?"

The answer formed directly in their minds: "I am **X**. I seek to destroy!"

"You can't. We'll find a way to stop you!"

Their heads rang with the Creature's inhuman laughter. "To banish me, you must know my number!" It folded its bandaged arms and waited.

The sides of the chamber began to glow. Lines and curves of golden light appeared. More numbers! There was an equation on each of the three blank walls. The first read:

$$3X - 7 + 5X + 9 = 66$$

Scullery found the route to tackle this equation. "It needs simplifying. If you put the X numbers together and the ordinary numbers together, you get

$$(+3X) + (+5X) + (-7) + (+9).$$

A plus times a minus equals a minus, so:

$$8X + 2 = 66.$$

If $8X = 66 - 2 = 64$, then

$X = 64 \div 8$, which comes to...."

"Don't say it!" Muldoon checked Scullery with a gesture. "Let's check it first. Look at the second equation."

The glowing figures on the second wall read:

$$3 (2X - 4) = 36$$

If Scullery was right, did this equation give the same value for **X**? Muldoon remembered that he had to multiply each term inside the bracket by the term outside it:

6X – 12 = 36

So **X = (36 + 12) 6 = 48 ÷ 6:** yes, that checked out!

Scullery, meantime, was solving the final equation:

–3 (6 – 4X) = 78

–3 x +6 = –18, she thought, and **–3 x –4X = 12 X,** because two minuses make a plus.
So, if **12X – 18 = 78,** then
12X = 78 + 18 = 96. Therefore, **X = 96 ÷ 12.**
The same answer again.

Sure of themselves now, Scullery and Muldoon turned to face their adversary.

"We have found your number, **X**. It is eight."

With a savage howl, the Creature disappeared in a vortex of searing light. From what strange, twisted dimension of Space or Time had it come?

Now, no-one would ever know.

Most innumerate
The Nambiquara people of the north-west Matto Grosso in Brazil lack any system of numbers. They do, however, have a verb which means 'they are alike'.

TOP ALGEBRA TIPS

Any collection of numbers or letters is called a TERM.

Which of the following are TERMS?

1) 4ab

2) 6y²

3) 6

4) 12 (4x + 7)

ANSWER: All of them!

OTHER THINGS TO REMEMBER ABOUT TERMS:

● All the letters and numbers in a term have to be multiplied or divided together.

● Terms are separated by + and - signs.

(Usually, the first term in an equation is given without a sign: any term without a sign is a PLUS.)

SIMPLIFYING is simply a matter of collecting like terms together:

eg 3y + 6 + 5y - 3 simplifies to

(3y + 5y) + (6 - 3) = 8y + 3

When you MULTIPLY OUT brackets, remember to multiply ALL the TERMS inside the brackets by the TERM outside.

THE NTH TERM

Once upon a time there was a guy who was stranded on a desert island. He loved figures and wanted to write a sequence he had dreamed up. Disaster struck! His last biro was running out!

His sequence was:

7   11   15   19   23

This was the cunning way he had made it:

1st term = 4 x 1 + 3 = 7
2nd term = 4 x 2 + 3 = 11
3rd term = 4 x 3 + 3 = 15

and so on...but he couldn't write it - no biro left. So he thought, "I'll make up a formula."

All he wrote was: 4n + 3

After 30 days he died of starvation. His maths friend found his body and his notebook with 4n + 3 written in it. So, on his gravestone he etched:

7   11   15   19   23...........123

This sad story (don't cry) goes to show that maths can keep you busy and happy on a desert island but it may not save your life.

Puzzled? 123 is the 30th term and it was put in because he died after 30 days.

THE MAGICAL FORMULA!

This formula describes sequences:

$$dn + (a - d)$$

Here is a sequence:

$$5 \quad 8 \quad 11 \quad 14$$
$$3 \quad 3 \quad 3$$

d = the "common difference" (three)
a = the "first term" or the first number in the sequence (five)
n stays as n

So, it goes like this:

3n + (5 - 3) which equals 3n + 2

That is your formula for the sequence!

If you don't understand, get help!
If you do understand, practise!

Some questions you might get asked about the Nth:

Find the 50th term of this sequence.

Put this sequence in a formula.

Put the 3rd term into a formula.

THE FAIRGROUND

Dice

You should know that the probability of getting a six on a 6 sided dice is $\frac{1}{6}$ because there are six sides on the dice so there are six possible outcomes. With two dice there are many more possible outcomes. Are there 12, 18, or 36?

The answer is 36 and if you haven't got anything to do for the next ten minutes, why don't you write them down on some paper. Start with 1, 1, then 1,2 until you get to 1,6 then start again at 2,1, etc.

Now add up the numbers $1 + 1 = 2$, $1 + 2 = 3$,...$1 + 6 = 7$ etc. Which number occurs the most?

It's seven isn't it? It occurs six times so the probability is $\frac{6}{36}$. What are the probabilities for the other numbers?

Lucky Dip

In the fairgound there is a lucky dip stall. It has a container and in this are different coloured discs. People pay 50p to pick out a coloured disc from sawdust and win different prizes depending on the disc they pick.

If there are 93 pink discs, 75 yellow discs and 32 black discs what is the probability of picking a disc of each colour?

Probability of pink = $^{93}/_{200}$

Probability of yellow = $^{75}/_{200}$

Probability of black = $^{32}/_{200}$

Probability oof a dis that is not yellow = $^{125}/_{200}$

What is my chance of winning the UK lottery?

"Millions to One!"

I hear you cry. Well, we can work it out.

There are 49 different balls, so the first number can be chosen in 49 different ways. This means that there are 48 balls left, so the second ball can be chosen in 48 ways. The third can be chosen in 47 ways, the fourth in 46 ways, the fifth in 45 ways and the sixth in 44 ways.

This means that there are 49 x 48 x 47 x 46 x 45 x 44 possible ways for the balls to come out. This is 100,683,475,520 ways.

But, as it doesn't matter in which order you have the balls when you fill in your ticket, there are 6 ways in which you choose the first number, 5 ways for the second and so on. So, there are 6 x 5 x 4 x 3 x 2 x 1 different ways to choose a winning ticket. This is 720 ways. So, your chance of winning the lottery is:

100683475520 – 720

= 13983816

(about 14 million to 1*!!*)

But people do win, don't they?

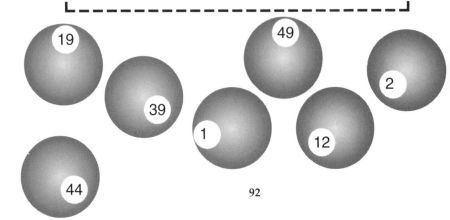

P.S. A cheerful note: if you bought a ticket on a Monday statistically you would be more likely to die in the following 5 days than to win the lottery!!

GET BETTER GRADES SURVEY

What do you do on a Friday night?

100 Get Better Grades readers were asked by Ivor Questions of the SORI Polls Organisation:

How do you spend Friday night?

Here are the results:
Watching TV: 15
With friend: 33
Grounded: 2
Cinema: 21
Opera: 1
Don't know: 28

What a boring list!

Get Better Grades shows you how to jazz up your presentation of information.

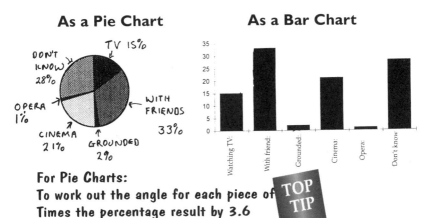

As a Pie Chart

TV 15%
DON'T KNOW 28%
OPERA 1%
CINEMA 21%
GROUNDED 2%
WITH FRIENDS 33%

As a Bar Chart

Watching TV; With friend; Grounded; Cinema; Opera; Don't know

For Pie Charts:
To work out the angle for each piece of
Times the percentage result by 3.6

TOP TIP

READERS SURVEY 2

We know all our readers are bright, witty, intelligent and perceptive because they've bought this book! However, we were curious to know how they differed in height and weight because we knew that some fuddy old examiner would ask a similar question.

So we asked 100 people to send in their statistics, but only 30 were willing to do so!

Here are the results: (top secret)

Height	Weight	Height	Weight
151	49	151	52
146	47	152	51
172	63	153	49
165	62	156	56
147	40	158	54
155	53	160	58
166	64	161	54
170	64	162	63
166	59	163	62
159	58	164	60
157	64	163	66
149	50	164	55
147	48	161	70
150	49	161	60
150	56		

There are a number of ways of communicating this information so that people can understand at a glance and summarise the information. For instance, here is a scatter graph:

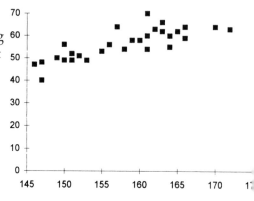

???

Conundrum:

Three people went into a hotel to book a room for the night. The night porter told them that they could have the room for £30.00, so they each gave him a tenner. An hour later, the night manager asked the porter about the room and, when he was told that the porter had let it out for £30.00, told him off and said that the room should have only cost £25.00. He insisted that the porter must return £5.00 to the occupants immediately. On his way up in the lift, the porter decided that the £5.00 couldn't be divided equally among the three guests, so he decided to give each of them £1.00 and keep the remaining £2.00 for himself. The guests were delighted to get a pound refund (thus only having paid £9.00 each) and the porter felt that receiving his £2.00 tip was fair enough, considering the extra work that he had to put in to get the guests their money back. Here is the conundrum that will drive your maths teacher crazy: Each guest has now paid £9.00 - nine times three = £27.00. The porter has kept £2.00. £27.00 + £2.00 = £29.00. The guests originally paid £30.00. WHERE'S THE MISSING POUND?

Here follows the reference section
TOP TIPS FOR EXAMS

Calculators: Standard or scientific - depending on your level. Bring one that you are familiar with and know how to use.

Revision: Start in good time. Do the maths from old papers and text books. Don't work for more than about an hour at a time. Show all your workings

Exam skills: Organise your time. Answer the easy questions first. Be aware of which questions can gain you the most marks. Show your workings. Check your answers

What to take: Calculator, batteries, pencil, sharpener, rubber, ruler, two pens plus cartridges, protractor, pair of compasses, set square, good luck gonk.

Types of question:

Short answer questions: Write the method, as well as the answer, and round off if necessary.

Structured questions: These questions use the answer on one question as part of the next question. It is very important that you show your method so that if you slip up in a small way the examiner will know what was going on in your mind when you get to the next question.

Combination questions: This type of question may require a short answer and the type of workings for a structured question.

Formulae sheets: When you go into an exam you will be given a sheet with equations which you are not expected to remember. Find out which equations they will give you and know how and when to use them.

INTERIOR AND EXTERIOR ANGLES

Using the rules you've come across you can work out the angles of a shape.

You'll probably be asked to work out the exterior and interior angles of a polygon.

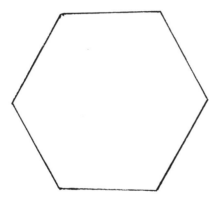

The exterior angle of a regular polygon can be worked out by using this formula:

Exterior Angle $= \dfrac{360°}{\text{The number of sides}}$

Therefore the exterior angles of the following shapes are:

Equilateral triangle $\dfrac{360°}{3} = 120°$

Square $\dfrac{360°}{4} = 90°$

Regular Pentagon $\dfrac{360°}{5} = 72°$

Regular Hexagon $\dfrac{360°}{6} = 60°$

Because we know that all degrees on a straight line add up to 180° (see page 00) the interior angles of a regular polygon can be worked out using this formula:

Interior angle = 180° – Exterior angle

So a regular hexagon's interior angles can be worked out like this:

180° – 60° (the exterior angle) = 120°

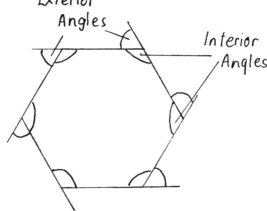

THESE RULES ARE BOUND TO HELP YOU WITH QUESTIONS ON SHAPE AND ANGLE!

STRAIGHT LINE GRAPHS

Here are some straight line graphs it would be useful to learn.

Y = X

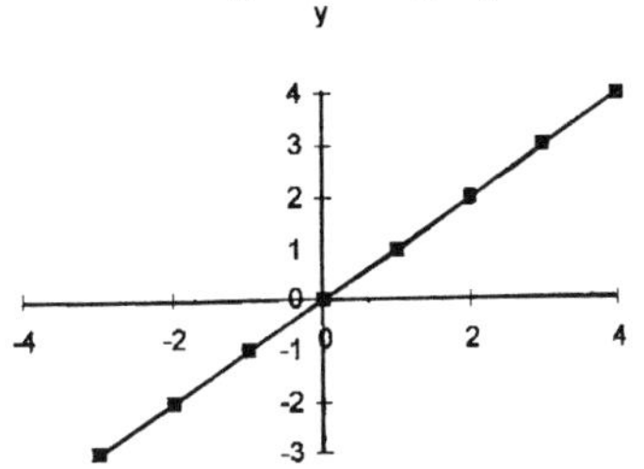

Y = -X

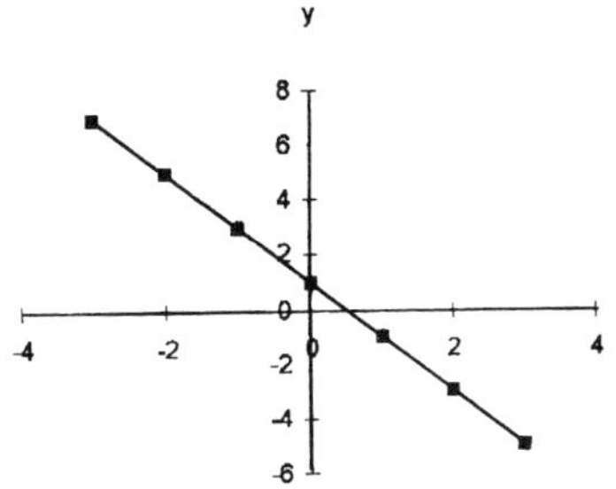

If you want to draw a straight line graph, you need to plot a table of values i.e.: Y = 2X

x	y
-3	0
-2	1
-1	2
0	3
1	4
2	5
3	6

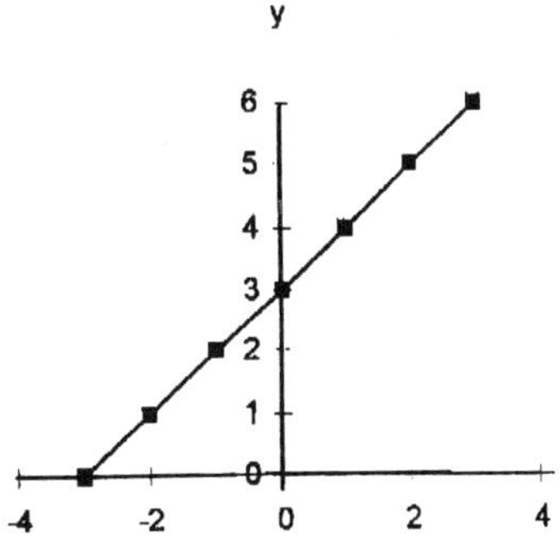

DO YOU KNOW WHAT Y = MX +C IS?
IT'S THE EQUATION OF A STRAIGHT LINE.

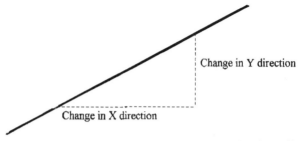

M is the gradient of the line. (Gradient can also be called slpe, steepness or incline.)

To find the gradient you need to draw a right-angled triangle underneath the line and work out the change in the X direction and the Y direction. Find the 'changes' by measuring the length of the lines. (Remember to look at the scale of the graph and count the squares on the graph paper. Don't use a ruler.)

GRADIENT = <u>Change in Y direction</u>
Change in X direction

Question:
Which line is steeper?
Y = 3X + 2 or Y = 5X + 2

Answer: Y = 5X + 2 as 5 is bigger than 3 (the gradient of the other graph.)

C i s the place were the line crosses the X axis.

GLOSSARY

Algebra:
Putting letters in place of numbers.

Angles,
Interior:The angles inside a shape.
Exterior: The angles outside a shape when the sides are extended.

Area:
The amount of space that is covered by a shape (2 dimensions)

Bearing:
An angle measure from a North line, always clockwise and written in three figures.

Circumference:
The distance around the outside of the circle.

Decimal places:
Number of places after the decimal point.

Diameter:
Distance from one side of a circle to the other through the centre.

Expand:
Remove brackets by multiplying.

Factor:
A number that divides into another number i.e. 6 is a factor of 12.

Perimeter:
The distance around the outside of a shape.

Pi:
The ratio between the circumference and diameter. Basically 3.14.

Probability:
The chance/likelihood of an event occurring.

Radius:
The distance from the centre of a circle to the circumference.

Ratio:
The relationship between one amount and another.

Scale factor:
The ratio by which you increase or decrease the picture/diagram.

Simplify:
Make easier/combine terms together.

Standard form:
Writing large or small numbers in powers of 10.

Symmetry,
Rotational: When you can turn a shape through an angle and it looks the same.
Reflectional: When you can place a mirror on a line and the shape looks the same on both sides.

Fraction	Decimal	Percentage
$\frac{1}{2}$	0.5	50%
$\frac{1}{4}$	0.25	25%
$\frac{3}{4}$	0.75	75%
$\frac{1}{3}$	0.333333	33%
$\frac{2}{3}$	0.666667	67%
$\frac{1}{10}$	0.1	10%
$\frac{2}{10}$	0.2	20%
$\frac{x}{10}$	0.X	X%
$\frac{1}{5}$	0.2	20%
$\frac{2}{5}$	0.4	40%

No	Square	Cube	Square root
1	1	1	1.000
2	4	8	1.414
3	9	27	1.732
4	16	64	2.000
5	25	125	2.236
6	36	216	2.449
7	49	343	2.646
8	64	512	2.828
9	81	728	3.000
10	100	1000	3.162
15	225	1375	3.873
20	400	8000	4.472
25	525	15625	5.000
30	900	27000	5.477
40	1600	84000	6.325
50	2500	125000	7.071

Index

Algebra, 32, 42, 85
Angles, 44
Area, 81

Bearings, 79
Bodmas, 13, 16, 19

Calculator, 12, 19, 61
Charts and graphs, 93, 99
Circles, 63
Common factors, 35
Confidence, 8

Decimals, 15, 31, 103

Exam tips, 96

Fractions, 15, 20, 103

Golden rules, 10
Graphs, 93, 99

Horoscopes, 12

Negative numbers, 14, 26
Number patterns, 23

Polygons, 40
Powers, 17
Prime numbers, 23
Probability, 90
Pythagoras, 69

Ratio, 54

Scale, 48
Sequences, 88
Shapes, 36
Significant figures, 29
Square and cube numbers,
        18, 24, 74, 103
Standard form, 17, 60
Symmetry, 77
Terms, 87
Time, 28
Triangles, 38

Volumes, 84

The X Files, 32, 42, 85